Drama for Students, Volume 12

Staff

Editor: Elizabeth Thomason.

Contributing Editors: Anne Marie Hacht, Michael L. LaBlanc, Ira Mark Milne, Jennifer Smith.

Managing Editor: Dwayne D. Hayes.

Research: Victoria B. Cariappa, *Research Manager*. Cheryl Warnock, *Research Specialist*. Tamara Nott, Tracie A. Richardson, *Research Associates*. Nicodemus Ford, Sarah Genik, Timothy Lehnerer, Ron Morelli, *Research Assistants*.

Permissions: Maria Franklin, *Permissions Manager*. Debra J. Freitas, Jacqueline Jones, Julie Juengling, *Permissions Assistants*.

Manufacturing: Mary Beth Trimper, *Manager, Composition and Electronic Prepress*. Evi Seoud, *Assistant Manager, Composition Purchasing and Electronic Prepress*. Stacy Melson, *Buyer*.

Imaging and Multimedia Content Team: Barbara Yarrow, *Manager*. Randy Bassett, *Imaging Supervisor*. Robert Duncan, Dan Newell, *Imaging Specialists*. Pamela A. Reed, *Imaging Coordinator*. Leitha Etheridge-Sims, Mary Grimes, David G. Oblender, *Image Catalogers*. Robyn V. Young, *Project Manager*. Dean Dauphinais, *Senior Image Editor*. Kelly A. Quin, *Image Editor*.

Product Design Team: Kenn Zorn, *Product Design Manager*. Pamela A. E. Galbreath, *Senior Art Director*. Michael Logusz, *Graphic Artist*.

Copyright Notice

Since this page cannot legibly accommodate all copyright notices, the acknowledgments constitute an extension of the copyright notice.

While every effort has been made to secure permission to reprint material and to ensure the reliability of the information presented in this publication, Gale neither guarantees the accuracy of the data contained herein nor assumes any responsibility for errors, omissions, or discrepancies. Gale accepts no payment for listing; and inclusion in the publication of any organization, agency, institution, publication, service, or individual does not imply endorsement of the editors or publisher. Errors brought to the attention of the publisher and verified to the satisfaction of the publisher will be corrected in future editions.

This publication is a creative work fully protected by all applicable copyright laws, as well as by misappropriation, trade secret, unfair competition, and other applicable laws. The authors and editors of this work have added value to the underlying factual material herein through one or more of the following: unique and original selection, coordination, expression, arrangement, and classification of the information. All rights to this publication will be vigorously defended.

Copyright ©2001
Gale Group, Inc.
27500 Drake Road
Farmington Hills, MI 48331-3535

All rights reserved including the right of reproduction in whole or in part in any form.

ISBN 0-7876-4086-7
ISSN 1094-9232

Printed in the United States of America.
10 9 8 7 6 5 4 3 2 1

Top Girls

Caryl Churchill 1982

Introduction

Since its earliest productions, Caryl Churchill's *Top Girls* was regarded as a unique, if difficult, play about the challenges working women face in the contemporary business world and society at large. Premiering on August 28, 1982, in the Royal Court Theatre in London before making its New York debut on December 28, 1982, in the Public Theatre, *Top Girls* won an Obie Award in 1983 and was the runner-up for the Susan Smith Blackburn Prize. The play is regularly performed around the world and has quickly become part of the canon of women's theater. *Top Girls* helped solidify Churchill's reputation as an important playwright.

Critics praise *Top Girls* for a number of reasons. Churchill explores the price of success paid for by the central character, Marlene, while using unusual techniques including a nonlinear construction, an overlapping dialogue, and a mix of fantasy and reality. The last occurs at a dinner party celebrating Marlene's promotion, which is attended by five women from different times in history, literature, and art. The dinner party is the first scene of the play and, to many critics, the highlight of *Top Girls*. Churchill brings up many tough questions over the course of the play, including what success is and if women's progress in the workplace has been a good or bad thing. While many critics compliment the play on its handling of such big ideas in such a singular fashion, some thought *Top Girls* was disjointed and its message muddled. As John Russell Taylor of *Plays & Players* wrote, "Like most of Churchill's work, it is about nothing simple and easily capsulated."

Author Biography

Churchill was born on September 3, 1938, in London, England, the daughter and only child of Robert Churchill and his wife. Churchill's father was a political cartoonist; her mother worked as a model, secretary, and actress. Churchill began writing stories and doing shows for her parents as a child. After spending her early childhood in London, the family moved to Montreal, Quebec, Canada, in about 1949, where Churchill spent most of her formative years.

In 1956, Churchill returned to England to enter Oxford University. While studying literature at Lady Margaret Hall, she began writing plays for student productions. Her first play was written as a favor for a friend. One of Churchill's student plays, *Downstairs*, won first prize at the National Student Drama Festival. Churchill graduated with her B.A. in 1960, intending to become a serious writer.

Family matters stymied her plans. In 1961, Churchill married David Harter, a lawyer, and had three sons over the next decade. Still, she managed to write about thirty radio dramas, usually one act, throughout the 1960s and early 1970s, as well as some television plays in the early 1970s. Many of these early plays were related to her life experiences and were somewhat depressing, but they did garner Churchill some notice for her writing abilities.

In the early 1970s, Churchill turned to theater,

initially writing for fringe theater groups. *Owners*, a tragic farce, was her first major play, produced by a fringe group in London in 1972. This production led to her position as a resident playwright at the Royal Court Theatre from 1974 to 1975. Churchill began exploring feminist ideas with her first play for the Royal Court, *Objections to Sex and Violence* (1974).

Churchill continued to explore feminism with *Vinegar Tom* (1976). She wrote the play both with the help of and for Monstrous Regiment, a feminist touring-theater company. *Vinegar Tom* and *Light Shining in Buckinghamshire* (1976) use historical settings to discuss repression. These plays garnered Churchill more attention and critical praise.

In 1979, Churchill's *Cloud Nine* had its first production. This was her first big hit, and had a long run on both sides of the Atlantic. The Obie Awardwinning play was set in the Victorian era, with the roles played by their physical opposites. For example, a man played an unhappy and unfulfilled wife. Critics enthusiastically praised Churchill's originality. Churchill followed this success with *Top Girls* (1982), a play about feminism and the price of success for women. Though some did not regard it as highly as *Cloud Nine*, the play cemented her reputation and won her another Obie.

Churchill wrote plays on a variety of topics throughout the 1980s and 1990s. *Fen* (1983), which focused on female tenant farmers, won her the Susan Smith Blackburn Prize. In 1986, she wrote

Serious Money about the London stock exchange. Churchill used music and dialogue that rhymed in the play, which also won the Blackburn Prize and many other awards. She continued to experiment with technique in *Mad Forest* (1990) and *The Skriker* (1994), which incorporated music and dance. Though Churchill's output decreased in the late 1990s, she continues to push the limits of traditional dramatic forms using dance and music, and other unexpected constructions.

Act 1, Scene 1

Top Girls opens in a restaurant where Marlene is hosting a dinner party for five friends. She has recently been promoted at work. The five guests are all women that are either long-dead or are fictional characters from literature or paintings.

The first to come are Isabella Bird and Lady Nijo. Nijo and Isabella discuss their lives, including their families. Dull Gret and Pope Joan, who was elected to the papacy in the ninth century, appear. The conversation wanders between subjects, including religion and the love lives of Nijo and Isabella. Isabella goes on about her travel experiences. Joan talks about dressing and living as a male from the age of twelve so that she could further her education. Marlene proposes a toast to her guests. They, in turn, insist on toasting Marlene and her success.

Joan relates her disturbing story. While she enjoyed being the pope, she also had a discreet affair with a chamberlain and became pregnant. In denial about her state, she gave birth to her child during a papal procession. Joan was stoned to death, and her child, she believes, was also killed. While Joan relates her story, Nijo talks about her four children being born, and only being able to see one of them after having given birth. Isabella talks about how she never had children. Marlene wonders why they are all so miserable.

The final guest arrives. She is Patient Griselda, a character in Geoffrey Chaucer's *The Canterbury Tales*. Griselda tells her story. Though she was a peasant girl, she was asked to be the wife of a local prince, but only if she obeyed him without question. Griselda agreed, though it later meant losing the two children she bore him—they were taken from her as infants. Then Griselda was sent back to her father with nothing but a slip to wear. Her husband called her back to help him prepare for his next wedding to a girl from France. The girl was her daughter—all this was a test of her loyalty. He took Griselda back, and the family was reunited.

Marlene is upset by Griselda's tale. Nijo is also perturbed because her children were never returned to her. Gret finally speaks up about her journey through hell, and how she beat the devils. The scene ends with Isabella talking about the last trip she took.

Act 1, Scene 2

The scene opens in the Top Girls employment agency in London. Marlene is interviewing Jeanine for possible placement. Marlene tells Jeanine that if she is to be sent on a job with prospects, she must not tell them that she is getting married or might have children. Marlene evaluates Jeanine and suggests jobs based on her perception of Jeanine's future.

Act 2, Scene 3

This scene takes place at night in Joyce's backyard in Suffolk. Joyce is Marlene's elder sister. Joyce's sixteen-year-old daughter Angie and her twelve-year-old friend Kit are playing in a shelter they built in the backyard. Joyce calls for Angie, but Angie and Kit ignore her until she goes back into the house. Angie says she wants to kill her mother.

Angie and Kit discuss going to the movies. Kit gets mad at Angie when she talks about dumb stuff. Angie desperately wants to leave home. Kit believes they should move to New Zealand in case of a war. Angie is indifferent because she has a big secret. She tells Kit she is going to London to see her aunt. Angie believes that Marlene is really her mother.

Joyce sneaks up on them. Joyce will not let them go to the movies until Angie cleans her room. Angie leaves, and Kit informs Joyce that she wants to be a nuclear physicist. When Angie returns, she is wearing a nice dress that is a little too small for her. Joyce becomes angry because Angie has not cleaned her room. It starts to rain. Joyce and Kit go inside. Angie stays outside. When Kit returns to get her, Angie threatens to kill her mother again.

Act 2, Scene 1

It is Monday morning at Top Girls. Win and Nell, who work at the agency, are talking. Win tells Nell about her weekend that she spent at her married boyfriend's house while his wife was out of town. The conversation turns to office gossip. They consider changing jobs as Marlene has been promoted over them, limiting their prospects. Still, Nell and Win are glad Marlene got the job over another coworker, Howard. Marlene enters late. Win and Nell tell her that they are glad she got the promotion rather than Howard.

Win interviews Louise, a forty-six-year-old woman who has been in the same job for twenty-one years. Louise has done everything for her company, but has spent twenty years in middle management with no opportunities to go higher. Win believes there will be only limited openings for her.

In the main office, Angie walks up to Marlene. Marlene does not recognize her at first. Angie has come to London on her own to see her aunt, and she intends to stay for a while. It is not clear if Joyce knows where Angie is. Angie becomes upset when Marlene does not seem like she wants her to stay.

Their conversation is interrupted by the appearance of Mrs. Kidd, Howard's wife. Mrs. Kidd is upset because Howard cannot accept that Marlene got the promotion to managing director over him. In part, he is disturbed because she is a woman. Mrs. Kidd wants Marlene to turn down the promotion so that he can have it. Mrs. Kidd leaves in a huff when Marlene is rude to her. Angie is proud of her aunt's saucy attitude.

In another interview, Nell talks to Shona, who claims to be twenty-nine and to have worked in sales on the road. As the interview progresses, it becomes clear that Shona has been lying. She is only twenty-one and has no real work experience.

In the main office, Win sits down and talks to Angie, who was left there by Marlene while she is working. Angie tells Win that she wants to work at Top Girls. Win begins to tell Angie her life story, but Angie falls asleep. Nell comes in and informs her that Howard has had a heart attack. When Marlene returns, Win tells her about Angie wanting to work at Top Girls. Marlene does not think Angie has much of a future there.

Act 2, Scene 2

This scene takes place a year earlier in Joyce's kitchen. Marlene is passing out presents for Joyce and Angie. One of the gifts is the nice dress that Angie wore in act 1, scene 2. While Angie goes to her room to try it on, Joyce and Marlene are talking. Joyce had no idea that Marlene was coming. Marlene believed Joyce had invited her there. Angie made the arrangements, lying to both of them.

Angie returns to show off the dress. They chide her for her deception. Angie reminds her that the last time she visited was for her ninth birthday. Marlene learns that Joyce's husband left her three years ago. It is getting late, and Angie is sent to bed. Marlene will sleep on the couch.

After Angie leaves to get ready for bed, Joyce and Marlene continue their discussion about their lives. The sisters' conversation turns into an argument. Marlene believes that Joyce is jealous of her success. Joyce criticizes the decisions Marlene has made, including leaving her home and giving up her child, Angie. Marlene offers to send her money, but Joyce refuses.

Marlene is excited about a future under the new prime minister, Margaret Thatcher, while Joyce cannot stand the prime minister. They talk about the horrid life their mother led with their alcoholic father. It becomes clear the sisters have very different views of the world. As Marlene nears sleep on the couch, Angie walks in, having had a bad dream. "Frightening," is all she says.

Characters

Angie

Angie is the sixteen-year-old adopted daughter of Joyce. Angie is the biological daughter of Marlene, but was given up by her birth mother, who was only seventeen at the time and had career ambitions. In act 1 of *Top Girls*, Angie realizes that Marlene is her mother, though she has not been told directly. Both Marlene and Joyce do not think highly of Angie and believe her future is limited. She has already left high school with no qualifications. She was in remedial classes, and her best friend is Kit, who is four years younger. Angie is frustrated and wants to murder her mother. Instead, she runs away to visit her aunt in London and hopes to live with her. Previously, Angie tricked Marlene into visiting her and Joyce. Angie is Marlene's embarrassment, but she is also one of the things that links her to the women at the dinner party.

Isabella Bird

Isabella is one of Marlene's dinner party guests in act 1, scene 1. She is a Scottish woman who lived in the late nineteenth and early twentieth centuries and who traveled extensively later in life. In *Top Girls*, Isabella is the first to arrive at the party and dominates the conversation in a self-absorbed manner. She talks on and on about her travels; her complex relationship with her sister, Hennie; her clergyman father, and husband; her illnesses; religion; and her lack of children. While Isabella does listen and respond to the others, she mostly tries to figure out her own life and what it meant. She could never be as good as her sister, but her adventures made her happy. Isabella is one of the characters who helps Marlene define herself.

Dull Gret

Dull Gret is one of Marlene's dinner guests in act 1, scene 1, and the third to arrive. Gret is the subject of a painting by Brueghel entitled "Dulle Griet." In the painting, she wears an apron and armor and leads a group of women into hell to fight with devils. Gret is generally quiet through most of the dinner, answering questions only when directly asked and making a few comments on the side. Near the end of the scene, Gret makes a speech about her trip to hell and the fight with the devils. Like all the dinner guests, Gret's story reflects something about Marlene's life.

Jeanine

Marlene interviews Jeanine for placement by Top Girls in act 1. She is engaged and is saving money to get married. Marlene is not supportive of Jeanine's ambitions to work in advertising or in a job that might have some travel, but she categorizes her according to what Marlene believes she will be able to accomplish.

Pope Joan

Pope Joan is one of Marlene's dinner party guests in act 1, scene 1, and the fourth to arrive. She is a woman from the ninth century who allegedly served as the pope from 854 to 856. Pope Joan is somewhat aloof, making relevant, intelligent declarations throughout the conversation. When the topic turns to religion, she cannot help but point out heresies—herself included—though she does not attempt to convert the others to her religion. Joan reveals some of her life. She began dressing as a boy at age twelve so she could continue to study; she lived the rest of her life as a man, though she had male lovers. Joan was eventually elected pope. She became pregnant by her chamberlain lover and delivered her baby during a papal procession. For this, Joan was stoned to death. At the end of the scene, Joan recites a passage in Latin. Like all the dinner guests, Joan's life and attitude reflects something about Marlene.

Joyce

Joyce is Marlene's elder sister and mother to Angie. Unlike her younger sister, Joyce stayed in the same area and social class she grew up in. Joyce is unambitious and unhappy. She was married to Frank, but she told him to leave three years previously because he was having affairs with other women. She supports herself and Angie by cleaning houses.

Because Joyce seemed to be unable to have children, she adopted Angie as an infant when Marlene decided to give her up. But Joyce soon got pregnant and miscarried the child because of the demands of raising Angie. Joyce resents both Angie and Marlene, in part because of her miscarriage. She calls Angie a lump and useless. Marlene is too ambitious and clever for Joyce.

Yet Joyce has pride. She will not take Marlene's money, and she does not cater to her crying. Joyce maintains her working class loyalty and stands her ground when Marlene starts to sing the praises of Margaret Thatcher. Despite such differences, Marlene and Joyce are very much alike. They both believe they are right and do what they must to survive in their different worlds.

Mrs. Kidd

Mrs. Kidd is the wife of Howard, the man who got passed over in favor of Marlene for the managing director position at Top Girls. In act 2, Mrs. Kidd comes to the office and tries to get Marlene to turn down the position. Mrs. Kidd hopes Marlene will understand how much it would hurt Howard's pride and livelihood. Marlene is not impressed by her pleas, and Mrs. Kidd leaves after insulting Marlene for being a hard, working woman.

Kit

Kit is the twelve-year-old best friend of Angie. Unlike Angie, Kit is clever and plans on being a nuclear physicist. The girls have been friends for years, though Kit gets annoyed by Angie's limitations. In some ways, Kit is a younger version of Marlene.

Louise

Louise is interviewed by Win for placement by Top Girls in act 2. Louise is a forty-six-year-old woman stuck in middle management who believes she has been overlooked for promotion and underappreciated by her present firm. Win is not particularly supportive of Louise's desires to use her experience elsewhere and does not offer much hope for a better position. Like Marlene, Win categorizes Louise according to what she believes Louise will be able to accomplish.

Marlene

Marlene is the central character in *Top Girls*. She is a successful businesswoman who has recently been promoted to managing director of Top Girls, an employment agency. To celebrate, she has a dinner party at a restaurant with five guests, all of whom are women who are either dead or fictional characters from literature and paintings. Marlene's own life shares some parallels with these women.

Marlene's adult life has been focused on her career, to the exclusion of nearly everything else.

She previously worked in the United States and has done well for herself. Marlene has little to no contact with her family. Her alcoholic father is dead, and her long-suffering mother is in some sort of home. Marlene does not get along with her sister Joyce, who has remained part of the working class and lives in the same neighborhood where they grew up.

Marlene let Joyce raise her daughter, Angie. Marlene became pregnant at age seventeen, and because the then-married Joyce did not have a child, she allowed her to adopt the baby. Marlene has as little respect and interest in Angie as Joyce does. Like the women she interviews at Top Girls, Marlene believes Angie's future is limited. Yet Marlene's own life is just as circumscribed, but in different ways. Her success has come at a high price, costing her both her empathy and her relationships.

Nell

Nell is one of the employees at the Top Girls employment agency. She is happy that Marlene got the promotion over Howard, but she has her own career ambitions and might want to find a job with better prospects. In the meantime, her boyfriend, Derek, has asked her to marry him, but she does not know if she will accept. Her career seems more important to her than the marriage. During the play, Nell conducts an interview with Shona, whom Nell believes might be good for Top Girls. Nell is disappointed to learn that Shona has lied about everything on her application.

Lady Nijo

Lady Nijo is one of Marlene's dinner party guests in act 1, scene 1, and the second to arrive. She is a thirteenth-century Japanese courtesan to the Emperor of Japan. She later became a Buddhist monk. Like Isabella, Nijo is somewhat self-absorbed, though not to the same degree. Nijo tells the others about her life, including information about her father, her lovers, her four children (only one of whom she ever saw), symbolic clothing, and her time as a traveling monk. But she also listens respectfully to the stories of others and acknowledges her limitations. Nijo liked her silk clothing and easy life with the Emperor. By the end of the scene, Nijo is in tears. Like all the dinner guests, Nijo's life reflects something about Marlene's.

Patient Griselda

Patient Griselda is one of Marlene's dinner guests in act 1, scene 1, and the last to arrive. She is a fictional character, appearing in "The Clerk's Tale" in Geoffrey Chaucer's *The Canterbury Tales*, among other stories. As soon as she arrives, Marlene has Griselda tell her story. Griselda was a peasant girl who was asked to marry a local prince, but only if she would obey him without question. She agreed and bore him two children who were taken away from her while they were still infants. She did not question the decision. Her husband sent Griselda back home with nothing more than a slip to wear. She went without question. He sent for her to help him plan his second marriage to a young French girl. Griselda came back. At a pre-wedding feast, he revealed that the girl and her page/brother were their children and all these incidents were tests of her loyalty. Like all the dinner guests, Griselda's story reflects an aspect of Marlene's life.

Shona

Shona is interviewed by Nell for placement by the Top Girls agency in the second act. Shona tries to pass herself off as a twenty-nine-year-old woman with sales experience, which Nell believes at first. As the interview progresses, it becomes clear that Shona has been making up a story. She is really twenty-one and has no job experience. Shona is certain that she could handle high-profile jobs, but Nell does not believe her.

Win

Win is one of the employees at the Top Girls employment agency. Like Nell, she is glad that Marlene got the promotion over Howard, but she has her own career ambitions and might move on. She is relatively well educated and has previously lived in several different countries. Win spent the previous weekend with her married boyfriend at his house, while his wife was out of town. During the course of the play, Win interviews Louise for a job; she shares Marlene's callous attitude toward Louise.

Choices and Consequences

Nearly every character in *Top Girls* has made or is in the process of making life-changing decisions with important consequences. The dinner party in act 1, scene 1 exemplifies this. Each of the historical figures has made a hard choice. For example, Pope Joan chose to live like a boy, and then a man, in public. When she became pregnant by her secret lover, the stoning death of her and her baby were consequences of her chosen life. Joyce chose to adopt Angie, which lead to a certain life path. Joyce believes that she miscarried her own child because of the demands of raising Angie.

Marlene also made several hard choices. She became a career woman who spent some time working in the States. Marlene is estranged from her family, including her biological daughter, Angie, and does not seem to have many close friends, female or male. Her dinner party in celebration of her promotion consists of women who are dead or do not really exist, not with friends or family. She has no love relationship. Marlene is very much alone because of her life choices. While her daughter Angie has already made two life choices— dropping out of school at the age of sixteen with no qualifications, and running away to London to live with her aunt/mother—the consequences of these actions in her life are unclear.

Success and Failure

Success is an important part of Marlene's life in *Top Girls*, defining who she is and whose company she enjoys. The dinner party is meant to celebrate her promotion to managing director as well as the successes of her guests. Joan became the pope. Isabella traveled the world. Gret fought the devils in hell. Griselda survived her husband's extraordinary tests of loyalty. Marlene sees these women as successful, though they are not in her real, everyday life. Marlene's personal life is a failure because of her success in business. She has no real friends in the play, and she has not seen her sister or biological daughter in seven years. At the dinner party, she moans at one point, "Oh God, why are we all so miserable?"

Yet, Marlene believes that Joyce is mostly a failure because she did not grow beyond her neighborhood; instead, she got married and raised a child. Joyce cleans houses for a living, and she is not impressed by Marlene's life. Joyce does not really see her world in the same terms of success or failure. She does what is necessary to survive and to rear Angie. However, both sisters agree that Angie has no chance of being a success in life. Angie has no education, no ambition, and is regarded as dumb. The best she might do is menial work and marry. While this describes Joyce's life, both Joyce and Marlene perceive that Angie might not be able to take care of herself. This would be the ultimate failure in their eyes. They agree that one should support oneself.

Topics for Further Study

- Research one of the five guests from history, literature, and art that come to Marlene's dinner party in act 1, scene 1 of *Top Girls*. Compare and contrast their lives to Marlene's life, focusing on issues of gender and success.

- Explore the psychological aspects of the complex relationship between Marlene, Joyce, and Angie. How could Marlene, Joyce, and Angie have avoided their sad situation?

- Research the state of the women's movement in Great Britain in the

1980s. Should Marlene be considered a feminist? Why or why not?

- Compare and contrast the public perception of Great Britain's prime minister in 1982, Margaret Thatcher, with Marlene. How were successful women viewed by society in this time period?

Class Conflict

Marlene and Joyce's differing definitions of success stem in part from a class conflict. Marlene has moved beyond her workingclass roots to a middle-class life by education and persistence. She holds a management position in a demanding field, an employment agency. She even lived and worked in the United States for several years. Marlene supports the political agenda of Great Britain's female prime minister, Margaret Thatcher, even though she is perceived as anti-workingclass.

Joyce remains firmly working class, leading a life only slightly better than her parents. She works as a cleaning lady to support Angie. Unlike Joyce and Marlene's mother, who stayed with her alcoholic husband and had nothing, Joyce told her husband to leave when she could no longer take his controlling nature and numerous affairs. Joyce regards Thatcher as evil, comparing her to Adolf Hitler, for her attitudes towards workingclass people. Joyce believes that Marlene thinks she is too good for her. Marlene says she does not like workingclass people, but she does not really include her sister as one of them. The pair never come to an understanding on class.

Sex Roles and Sexism

Throughout the text of *Top Girls* is an implicit discussion on what society expects women to be. Each of the guests at the dinner party defines womanhood in a particular era, either by what they are or by what they are not. Isabella, for example, could not live up to the standards of femininity defined by her sister, Hennie. Yet Isabella was a traveler who saw more of the world than most men. Marlene also breaks out of the traditional roles for women, by virtue of her career.

While Marlene has benefited economically from her career, her disregard for sex roles has its problems. She is not married, and it does not seem like she is in a long-term relationship. Joyce does not really like her. Mrs. Kidd, the wife of the man who was passed over for the promotion that Marlene got, begs her to not take it. Mrs. Kidd believes that the upset Howard should not have to work for a woman. Further, Mrs. Kidd hopes that Marlene will give up the promotion because Howard has to support his family. Mrs. Kidd calls Marlene "unnatural" for her uncompromising stand on the promotion and her attachment to her job. Marlene does not give in, but such sexism does not make her life and choices any easier.

Setting

Top Girls is a feminist drama/fantasy set in contemporary times. The action is confined to two places in England, London and Suffolk. The realistic action takes place in two settings. One is the Top Girls employment agency, where Marlene works. There, potential clients are interviewed, and Angie shows up, hoping to stay with Marlene. The other is Joyce's home and backyard, where Marlene visits and Angie and Kit scheme. The fantasy dinner party that opens Top Girls also takes place in London. (In many productions, the restaurant is called La Prima Donna.) Though the dinner is clearly a fantasy because all the guests are dead or fictional, the setting is very real.

Fantasy versus Reality

In act 1, scene 1, Marlene hosts a dinner party with guests both long dead (Pope Joan, Lady Nijo, and Isabella Bird) and fictional (Dull Gret and Patient Griselda). While Marlene listens to and guides the conversation—injecting only bits about herself—these five women share their stories. The party is ostensibly to celebrate Marlene's promotion at work, but she intends it to be a celebration of all their successes. Though these women have each achieved something they are proud of, success has come at a large price in their lives. The dinner party itself shows the tensions between fantasy and reality because the guests are not "real" to the rest of the characters in *Top Girls*, only to Marlene. Yet the ideas and problems brought up by the fantasy women are very real. These issues echo in the plot and dialogue of the rest of the text, adding another dimension to the tension between fantasy and reality.

Time

Top Girls is not a linear play, but one in which time is used in an unusual fashion. The last scene of the play, act 2, scene 2, is the only part that takes place at a specific time in the story, about a year earlier than the other events. This flashback ties up some of the loose ends created by the story. The rest of the scenes, even the action within act 2, scene 1, do not have to take place in the order presented, though all are set in the present. The events are linked thematically, but not by a specific sequence of time. In addition, the idea of time is toyed with at the dinner party in act 1, scene 1. None of the guests can really exist at the same time, yet they share many of the same concerns.

Multiple Casting

Often when *Top Girls* is performed—including its premieres in England and the United States— several parts are played by the same actresses. Only the actress who plays Marlene, the central character in the play, has only one role. Thus guests at the dinner party are played by actresses who also play contemporary characters. Such casting decisions create visual links between seemingly disparate women. In the original production, for example, the same actress played Dull Gret and Angie, implying that these characters might have something in common. Similarly, another actress took on the roles of Pope Joan and Louise, drawing another parallel. This casting technique further emphasizes how alike the concerns of the historical characters and contemporary characters really are.

Historical Context

In the early 1980s, Great Britain was ruled by women. Though Queen Elizabeth II was only a royal figurehead, real political power was held by Prime Minister Margaret Thatcher. A member of the Conservative Party, Thatcher had been elected on May 3, 1979, and proceeded to put her own stamp on British life over the next decade or so. She was reelected in 1983 and 1987, and held office until late 1990, when she received a vote of no confidence and was replaced by fellow Conservative John Major. Thatcher had been the longest serving prime minister in Great Britain since the nineteenth century.

To improve the British economy, Thatcher dismantled the socialist practices that were put in place in the post-World War II era. She privatized major industries, like coal mining and telecommunications, which had been run by the British government, and she cut down on the power of trade unions. Because Thatcher's revolution benefited the middle-and upper-classes and seemed to hurt the working-and lower-classes, she was very unpopular among the latter groups. Unemployment continued to rise, and by 1982, over three and a quarter million people were unemployed. With cuts in both welfare and other social programs, such people's lives were becoming much harder. Though the economy was strong and interest rates and inflation were down, real living standards had been falling slightly for several years; international trade was also down.

In 1982, Thatcher and the Conservative party had some popularity problems among the general population. National morale was not particularly high until the Falklands War broke out. The Falkland Islands were a British possession in the Atlantic Ocean off the coast of Argentina. The group of islands are small and only about 1,800 people were living there. The territory was at the center of a dispute between Argentina and Great Britain for a number of years, and the two countries were in negotiations over them. In the spring of 1982, Argentina became impatient and invaded the Falklands. Great Britain responded and reclaimed the islands before Argentina quickly surrendered. Though there were approximately 243 British casualties, the victory improved national moral and the repute of Thatcher and the Conservatives. The popularity of the Labour party went down.

Thatcher was but one symbol in the 1980s of powerful women. There was a concrete change in the position of working women. In Great Britain in the early 1980s, women made up forty percent of the labor force, and over sixty percent of women aged twenty to sixty-four were working. Marriage rates fell in the 1980s, after having remained stable for many years. Before that decade nearly every adult woman was married at some point. Those that did marry gave up working after having a child, although sometimes they went back to work after their children went to school or reached adulthood.

Most women who worked were employed in poorly paid white collar, service, and industrial occupations. Approximately seventy-five percent of women did personal services work, clerical work, retail work, or health, education, or welfare work. The number of professional women was still small, but more women were becoming lawyers than ever before. These professional women often had equal pay for equal work, but working class women did not. Despite the success of Thatcher, many British women were anti-Conservative, though they did not necessarily support Labour either. To these women, Thatcher may have shared their gender, but her political prominence did not necessarily make her their heroine.

Critical Overview

Most critics agree that *Top Girls* is an intricate play; generally, they find much to praise in its themes, attitudes, and text. The play's depiction of women and feminism is particularly interesting to critics.

Compare & Contrast

- **1982:** Great Britain is led by a female Conservative prime minister, Margaret Thatcher, who was regarded as harsh.
  Today: Great Britain is ruled by a male Labour prime minister, Tony Blair, who is regarded as personable.

- **1982:** Great Britain goes to war with Argentina over possession of the Falkland Islands and wins.
  Today: The Falkland Islands are still a British protectorate, but self-governing. The citizens have been under constant British military protection ever since the war.

- **1982:** A "have-it-all" concept of life is common for women in the United States and Great Britain. Many strive for wealth, a successful career, and a perfect family.
  Today: While material and personal

success are still important, a more realistic tone predominates as the difficulties of trying to balance it all are realized.

- **1982:** The feminist movement is floundering in Great Britain and the United States. The agenda of many feminist organizations has little to do with the reality of the lives of ordinary women. In the United States, this trend is symbolized by the failure to ratify the Equal Rights Amendment to the Constitution.

  Today: In a post-feminist society, women's organizations regroup to address concerns of women of different classes. In 1998 in the United States, the National Council of Women's Organizations (representing six million women) drafts potential legislation for the National Women's Equality Act, which calls for the end of sex discrimination.

Writing about the original London production, Bryan Robertson of *The Spectator* argued, "her play is brilliantly conceived with considerable wit to illuminate the underlying deep human seriousness of her theme. The play is feminist, all right, but it is an entertaining, sometimes painful and often funny play and not a mere tract." Expanding on this idea,

Benedict Nightingale of the *New Statesman* wrote, "What use is female emancipation, Churchill asks, if it transforms the clever women into predators and does nothing for the stupid, weak and helpless? Does freedom, and feminism, consist of aggressively adopting the very values that have for centuries oppressed your sex?"

Writing about the same production, John Russell Taylor of *Plays & Players* is one of several critics over the years who believed that the rest of *Top Girls* did not live up to the promise of the dinner party scene. He found the play disjointed, arguing that "the pieces in the puzzle remain determinedly separate, never quite adding up to more than, well, so many fascinating pieces in a fascinating puzzle."

When *Top Girls* opened in the United States a short time later, a few critics were dismissive of the play and Churchill's potential appeal to American audiences. Calling the play "confused," Douglas Watt of the *Daily News* proclaimed, "Churchill can write touchingly and with a good ear for everyday speech about middle-class Londoners today. But while concern for ugly ducklings may be universal . . . *Top Girls* is a genre piece likely to arouse even less interest here than Alan Ayckbourn's equally tricky, but infinitely more amusing, works about the English middle class."

Edith Oliver of the *New Yorker* was perplexed by certain aspects of the play. She wrote "*Top Girls*. . . is witty and original, with considerable dramatized feeling, yet somehow never got to me, and I was never certain whether she was making one point with the whole play or a lot of points in its separate segments." Later in her review, Oliver emphasized that "[d]espite my admiration of Miss Churchill's ingenuity, I was disappointed and at times puzzled—never quite certain, for exampie, whether the historical characters of the first scene were meant to be the prototypes of modern characters. . . ."

A majority of American critics commented on the uniqueness of certain aspects of *Top Girls*, but they were most concerned with its feminist theme and social meanings. For example, John Beaufort of the *Christian Science Monitor* called *Top Girls* "a theatrical oddity in which the long view of what has been happening to womankind's 'top girls' combines with a sharp look at contemporary women achievers and a compassionate glance at the plight of an underclass underachiever who will never know the meaning of room at the top. Apart from one cheap shock effect, Miss Churchill has written a thoughtful and imaginative theater piece."

Along similar lines, T. E. Kalem of *Time* asks in his review, "Is the future to be divided between a smart, scrambling upper class of no-holds-barred individualists and a permanent underclass of poor souls who are unfit for the survival of the fittest?" An unnamed reviewer in *Variety* added, "If it's about male manipulation, *Top Girls* also pointedly involves the conditioned mentality of the sisterhood itself, with its inherited sense of role in a masculine or at least male-dominated world. The play seems to be saying that women historically have had themselves as well as sexist pigs for enemies." John Simon of *New York* believes the ideas in *Top Girls* have universal applicability. "This is not easy theater, but funny, fiercely serious, and greatly worth thinking about. Its aporias [insoluble contradictions] are not only pertinent to women, they also concern the entire, always incomplete, human condition."

Top Girls has continued to be performed regularly over the years. Most critics believe the play has withstood the test of time, despite specific references to British prime minster Margaret Thatcher and attitudes specific to the early 1980s. Of a 1991 revival in London, Paul Taylor in *The Independent* argued, "What continues to distinguish *Top Girls* is its cool, objective manner. The scenes in the job agency are almost too cleverly efficient in the way they expose the heartlessness the women have had to assume along with their crisp power-outfits. Churchill permits you to identify with the tricky plight of these characters but she does not ask you to like them." Similarly, Alastair Macaulay of the *Financial Times* believes, "Both as theatre and as politics, *Top Girls* is exciting and irritating. The dialectic of its final scene, between the Thatcherite Marlene and her socialist sister Joyce rings true as you listen. The terms in which the sisters argue about Thatcherite politics have not dated."

What Do I Read Next?

- *Cloud 9* is a play by Churchill written in 1979. Like *Top Girls*, this play is experimental in form and characterizations and includes feminist themes.

- *Skirmishes*, a drama written by Catherine Hayes in 1982, also concerns two sisters conflicted over family matters.

- *Steaming* is a feminist play by Nell Dunn written in 1981. It is from the same era as *Top Girls*, and has themes similar to *Top Girls*.

- *Ugly Rumors*, a drama about Margaret Thatcher and other British prime ministers, was written by Tariq Ali and Howard Bronton in 1998. The play concerns the differences in the interactions between Thatcher and male prime ministers.

- *Objections to Sex and Violence* is a play by Churchill first produced in 1975. At the center of the drama is a tense relationship between two very different sisters.

- *The Feminine Mystique*, written by Betty Friedan and originally published in 1963, was one of the first important books addressing the issues of equality for women. Since its first printing, Friedan's book has inspired and encouraged women as they have sought to establish careers, widen their presence in the business world, and create a fulfilling home life. The reissued edition, published in 1984, features a new introduction and speaks to topics that are of particular interest to women today, including health insurance, welfare reform, sexual harassment and discrimination, the growing presence of women in sports, and the decreasing wage gap between men and women.

Sources

Barnes, Clive,"Wry *Top Girls* is Hard to Top," in *New York Post*, December 29, 1982.

Beaufort, John, "Innovative Guests from the Royal Court: *Top Girls*," in the *Christian Science Monitor*, January 3, 1983, p. 15.

Churchill, Caryl, *Top Girls*, Methuen, 1982.

Kalem, T. E., Review in *Time*, January 17, 1983, p. 71.

Macaulay, Alastair, Review in The *Financial Times*, April 17, 1991, section l, p. 13.

Nightingale, Benedict, "Women's Playtime," in *New Statesman*, September 10, 1982, p. 27.

Oliver, Edith, "Women's Affairs," in The *New Yorker*, January 10, 1983, p. 80.

Review in *Variety*, September 8, 1982, p. 116.

Robertson, Bryan, "Top-Notch Churchill," in *The Spectator*, September 11, 1982, p. 25.

Shirley, Don, "*Top Girls* Wins Sympathy for Britain's Lower Echelons," in *Los Angeles Times*, January 30, 1998, p. 6.

Simon, John, "Tops and Bottoms," in *New York*, January 10, 1983, p. 62.

Stevens, Lianne, "*Top Girls* Gets Lost in Shuffle," in *Los Angeles Times*, August 12, 1986, part 6, p. 1.

Taylor, John Russell, Review in *Plays & Players*, No. 350, November 1982, pp. 22-3.

Taylor, Paul, "Presciently Tough at the Top," in *The Independent*, April 16, 1991, p. 14.

Watt, Douglas, "British *Top Girls* Not for U.S.," in *Daily News*, December 29, 1982.

Further Reading

Ashton, Elaine, *Caryl Churchill*, Northcote House, 1997.

>This is a critical study of the whole of Churchill's catalog, including *Top Girls*.

Bruley, Sue, *Women in Britain Since 1900*, Macmillan, 1999.

>This social history of British women includes information about the 1980s.

Gilmour, Ian, *Dancing with Dogma: Britain Under Thatcherism*, Simon & Schuster, 1992.

>This is an economic and political history of the Great Britain that *Top Girls* is set in.

Kritzer, Amelia Howe, *The Plays of Caryl Churchill: Theatre of Empowerment*, Macmillan, 1991.

>This book is a critical overview of and commentary on Churchill's work, including *Top Girls*, radio plays, and television plays.

Thompson, Juliet S. and Wayne C. Thompson, eds., *Margaret Thatcher: Prime Minister Indomitable*, Westview Press, 1994.

This collection of essays considers the whole of Thatcher's life and political career.

Lightning Source UK Ltd.
Milton Keynes UK
UKHW021023190922
409092UK00010B/926

9 781375 395120